SIX GREAT PIANO SONATAS

Wolfgang Amadeus
MOZART

DOVER PUBLICATIONS, INC.
Mineola, New York

Bibliographical Note

This Dover edition, first published in 2003, is a new compilation of works originally published in Series 20, "Sonaten und Phantasien für das Pianoforte" of Mozart's Complete Works Edition, originally published by Breitkopf & Härtel, Leipzig [1877-83]. The contents listing, main headings, and English footnotes are newly added.

International Standard Book Number: 0-486-42662-9

Manufactured in the United States by Courier Corporation
42662903
www.doverpublications.com

CONTENTS

● Mozart's works, including the piano sonatas in this collection, are identified by their numbers in Ludwig Köchel's *Chronological-Thematic Catalog* of the composer's works (1862). Later editions radically altered the "K" numbering of some of the pre-1784 works, based on later documentation. For example, the Sonata in A Minor, traditionally listed as K310, now carries the revised number K300d. Where two numbers exist, this Dover edition lists both, with the original given first. ● For Nos. 10, 11 and 12, *Grove* differs from all other authorities, giving a later date of 1781-3. ● The precise composition dates for No. 14 and No. 16 are taken from Mozart's own handwritten catalog, begun in 1784. ● The celebrated Sonata in C Major, K545, may appear as either No. 15 (Breitkopf edition) or No. 16 (Nathan Broder's Presser edition, 1956).

SONATA No. 8 IN A MINOR

K310 / 300d

[Early summer 1778, Paris]

4   Sonata No. 8 in A Minor *(K310)*

6   Sonata No. 8 in A Minor *(K310)*

Andante cantabile con espressione.

Sonata No. 8 in A Minor *(K310)* 13

14 Sonata No. 8 in A Minor *(K310)*

SONATA No. 10 IN C MAJOR
K330 / 300h
[Summer 1778 / or 1781–3, Munich or Vienna?]

18   Sonata No. 10 in C Major *(K330)*

Andante cantabile.

*) Das Folgende befindet sich nicht im Original-Manuscript, wohl aber in allen, auch den ältesten Ausgaben.
[The following does not appear in the original MS, but it does in all editions, even the earliest.]

22 Sonata No. 10 in C Major *(K330)*

Allegretto.

26   Sonata No. 10 in C Major *(K330)*

SONATA No. 11 IN A MAJOR

K331 / 300i

[Summer 1778 / or 1781–3, Munich or Vienna?]

VAR. VI.
Allegro.

MENUETTO.

Alla Turca.
Allegretto.

SONATA No. 12 IN F MAJOR

K332 / 300k

[Summer 1778 / or 1781–3, Munich or Vienna?]

44   Sonata No. 12 in F Major *(K332)*

(Nach den ältesten Ausgaben) [According to the earliest editions]

(Nach dem Autograph Mozart's) [According to Mozart's MS]

46   Sonata No. 12 in F Major *(K332)*

54 Sonata No. 12 in F Major *(K332)*

SONATA NO. 14 IN C MINOR

K457

[14 October 1784, Vienna]

58 Sonata No. 14 in C Minor *(K457)*

Adagio.

(sotto voce)

(Die eingeklammerten Vortragsbezeichnungen gemäss den ältesten Ausgaben, das Autograph
enthält, deren nur bei den Variationen des Themas und im Coda.)

[The performance indications in parentheses follow the earliest editions;
the MS contains some only in the variations of the theme and in the coda.]

Molto allegro.

(Nach den ältesten Ausgaben.) [According to the earliest editions]

(Nach dem Autograph.) [According to the MS]

legato

66   Sonata No. 14 in C Minor *(K457)*

Sonata No. 16 in C Major

K545

[26 June 1788, Vienna]

72 Sonata No. 16 in C Major *(K545)*

RONDO.
Allegretto.

76 Sonata No. 16 in C Major *(K545)*